for Roland & Anna

Peter Dent

best wishes always,

Peter Dent

Selected previous publications by Peter Dent:

Poetry

Simple Geometry (Oasis Books, 1999)
At the Blue Table (Blackthorn Press, 1999)
Settlement (Ferne Press, 2001)
Unrestricted Moment (Stride, 2002)
Adversaria (Stride, 2004)

As editor

The Full Note: Lorine Niedecker (Interim Press, 1983)
Not Comforts // But Vision : Essays on the Poetry of George Oppen
(Interim Press, 1985)
Candid Fields: Essays and Reflections on the Work of Thomas A. Clark
(Interim Press, 1987)

Handmade Equations

Poems 2000-2004

Peter Dent

Shearsman Books
Exeter

First published in the United Kingdom in 2005 by
Shearsman Books
58 Velwell Road
Exeter EX4 4LD

www.shearsman.com

ISBN 0-907562-65-5

Front cover illustration by the author.

Acknowledgements

Some of these poems have previously appeared in the following
magazines, often in earlier versions.

Poetry Salzburg Review, Stride, Tears in the Fence, Wandering Dog.

The author wishes to thank the editors for their support.

CONTENTS

HORIZONS AND FAÇADES

FAITH AND VALEDICTION

At times it seems to me
that, between us, there is
the confused memory
of mutual crimes.

Here we are projected face to face
for understanding.

Guillevic, *Carnac*
(tr. Teo Savory)

Horizons and Façades

NEW REGISTER

Smouldering   the new blues attaching themselves
To Autumn hills where his someone watches   as
Always   anxious at the wheel of an empty sky

His words   more likely to turn a fortune in
Its quick immaculate machinery   and its gratis
Invitation to nothing else   he knows it knows

Himself the demand lies elsewhere   seeing over
The hills what looks like trouble   skies burning
Up with promise   familiar easy roads now just

Impossible to read   he'll not be finished so easily
His starmaps left for night   for love left partly
Consummated   too immaterial an illusion trying

To see him off and minus belief   it's easy if
Still an interim account   the answers trickling in
To a natural lake   come October reconstructed

Asking to see it out   woods high on the skyline
Find him dreaming up the marvellous   extremes
Of chance   he's steering clear he's ready to go

MAKING A CLEARING

Memory   nothing now I consider it   registers
This garden's a fine creation   the colours track
Mad circuits   to repeat   and repeat me briefly

Handing over the fine control whose better day
Works up and over fiction   sparkling any blues
And silvers even out of a mystery   a palette

To turn your head   more things than can guess
What's next   I ask you   taking everything in
Hand   love's undercover situation   do broader

Headlines occupy more space   time's up   just
Look   how opening a thousand heads to colour
I quit   this minute's wild-eyed editorial may

Make for better style   live petals ever the worse
And maybe better for wearing out   choice dazzler
Can you sign this register again   before you go

Repeat   and repeat me things that every garden
Knows   my season's asking who steals who
Evaluates do I   self-regulate belief   its flower

WHICH DAYS

Which context are we speaking of   a strong
And unsubstantiated wind   and flash of light
To pray for a safe return   there was nothing

To it said the correspondent   I am part and
Parcel of the 'whole darn thing'   discretion?
Still worse than visible revenue   it's a world

Out there of colour   distressed or polished up
Persuasion   today there's a spring in my step
Like yesterday   imagination turned out wholly

Other   and complete   he heard the first and
Then the second explosion   masonry   glass
Mid-city deserts   no going back but glances

Your cautious eye   like every yesterday I've
Yet to know   (say when)   keeps pouring in
And sparkling   no-one's to know how long

Impressions last   to think who could've been
There   reigning grief   a distance in the thick
Of it   whose skin is golden   fragile   stay

ONLY AN EVERYDAY CONCOCTION

Flashlight   memory knows the perfect interval
Down a trail   flicks switches   sometimes for
Sorrow and sometimes who can guess its game

Misplaces a shine   renewing   in a landscape
The least familiar figure   skyline silvery quick
To a quandary   has the restless day go down

In words   to love?   as random as a word is
Often disengaged like an apparition I've mislaid
Examines in absentia rudimentary gold   hours

Hanging on   to hang on but they can't be told
Too smoky-smudged for an oakwood   nothing
Is ever at our beck and call   come in   it may

Invite   for sleep to lose more yesterdays than
Time   and so it goes   holds nothing against
One shadow sworn to fade   days just a place

To get things done   leaves weather a sky   to
Wholeness   gales of the 'great thing coming'
Watch   how resolution finds us   playing up

DREAMED-OF EXTREMES

questions on a day out

Description?   something there   in the counting out
Of things   what actually is   whether you like it or
Not makes up a 'fullness' for the intellect   of sorts

Grand colours working a line through mental weather
Chiselling out a decent angle   that avenue   or this
Taking a walk through the park   hearing the singing

Singing the birds   outlandish almost turquoise trees
In a certain kind of light   you know you have to be
Full grown to measure   and how much time?   your

Statement's calm   controlled   in its white quotidian
Way I am concerned   who's asking the question here
When I'm much more into play than yesterday   I

Looked the part   all right   an average passing eye
And getting square with the world   more often even
Unphasing   its rags and bobtails of off-white clouds

But propriety?   and nothing worked for   just that
Sense of possibility the last hours of a maze   worth
What?   good reason's smiling   it makes you think

COMING ON ORDER

and cannot say

Given to understand a little local colour to find
Myself a minor place   unearned with deep shade-
Driven buttercups   memories climbing the higher

The look there bright on your face   subliminal
Equations for how amazed the world is dreaming
The figures I needed to know   at last complete

In a stream of instant daybreaks firing   perhaps
Attenuated perhaps disrupted with absurd delight
Some other 'beingness' on call   its yes to enquiry

Asks me am I breathing   taking a second breath
To feel the secret weather loaded in it   still no
Meaning gives the game away   just one   I mean

The wildest takes it easy   though unknown it's
Better known to some   if preternaturally bound
To light the fuse   imagination turning into world-

Wide riot   whose future can't reread the present
Tense   its every power line energising all the
Dark I'm touching   if nothing ever   total earth

LOGBOOK CRAZY

and talking it up

Today this week or next   the weather calls
Another truth to order   its convoys moving
Steadily out of town   quite violent company

Despatching words   if only after dark   such
Lavish industry would work   involve myself
Obedient to occasion   a metaphor for once

Left out the picture   and calling the shots ...
Companions of honour do I mix it   all that
Light for now   in a field's explosive places

Mapping the unsold text   reluctantly in time
Moved off   through barbed wire as another
A black word said   more zeros in the mouth

Where paras head for psalms   tomorrow say
And the sentence after   after this   don't let
High Summer mess with individual nature ...

Engagements off   and the guns go quiet
Last duty: get the bloody thing discharged
Let even the dirtiest cloud select its hour

OF FAILING INTEREST

'Be there'   be prone to such an order   and daring?
Not that I'd intercede on a day like this   or do I
Entertain such brazen skies   make this or whatever

The last time seem enough   exceptional on its own
That you put it down to 'business acumen'   okay
In the circumstances   cloudless   as Midsummer

Day repeats itself sees everything in clover   heavens
You say   but you hadn't a prayer or escape   left
Only this   the chaotic and half-constructed empire

You'd unhinged   whose was whose is it   nobody's
Fault but mine   turns a late night conversation
Down on its luck   till a new day burns   dictating I

Read you   hard like most good stories   demanding
A presence   an offhand twinkling of an eye a gleam
On blackthorn?   even odder day-to-day phenomena

The half-right word   in its mobile hinterland its
Deep interior   darker than you think   I'm proving
Everything is special   if only when it's through

PRE-WINTER MANIFEST

Night with its overdose   its electrons crowding
The circuit   so life's but once too memorable
A window overgrown   for paradox   too bright

Blues in a sudden band   an envelope   whatever
Registers enough is sure to be contained   there's
No persuading   what stops what leaves its trace

An eye for shadow?   not looking for reasons
Even rests its case   here's willing all across my
Spectrum   oh any gleam can settle out of court

Headlights and rain   in mind   and then to see
What answers turn away in two dimensions there
It's something and nothing   precious in the air

The verb 'to bear' repeats itself   no stopping
The red reminder   was it yesterday   that now
Plays up   good grace is actual   knows its place

Another field it was   resolved and not the first
Time saved   these maples   hard along the edge
The traffic   all of its shifting   amplifying red

SCHEMA AND DEPARTURE

thinking on W.B.

As Summers go   as Summers in their likeness
Go   and nothing slowly   leap by leap   this
Side of heaven's swallows in their 'heaven' turn

For home   then anything I say and do I say it
Will be out of some peculiar dark gravity   down
To you   *subtending* — tell me how — what

Apparatus? not something I claim to know
I'm hazy still about the deal it takes   to raise
A cloud   its like unmade enough I dare to speak?

Not thinking even and some say better so   long
Lives condensed   we're quickly into it   like
Metaphor?   to find ourselves   'constructed'

Dropping shadows out of shadow   whereby this
My thin excuse   *un*minded   taking it all to heart
To open up a line   unstable but exquisite cloud:

Use additives   judiciously   whatever the word
Says aren't we just the end   give me a call when
Skies come clear   look up   download this flight

ELIMINATION

In extremis apprehension   conducting but only
After failing the miraculous   his new all-weather
Unrepeatable experiment   takes flask and burner

Clouds   does he distinguish?   sees what maybe
There is happening to notes   the violent instant
In and raiding chance   its anti-theft design   as

Gulls come hurtling free by choice   to recognise
The all too obvious   in thinking   why the gulls
Why cloud   more choice mark time   he knows

For sure the standard mystery   can answer it
Slick wings?   a pure white metaphor?   come
Daylight running it out of town   repressive

Truth   well it's conclusive   where he goes
He must manoeuvre   try out non-relationships
His lab extends   to observe what's left to play

With   heady in extremis blue   free-ranging light
Through glassware bubbling   bearable but only
Just   alliterate as he would have it   ready fumes

ODD DETAIL (AND MEMORANDUM)

Being not about time   and me to inherit a wood
Avoiding the displacing of an emptiness   I saw
More truth shot through with futures than any

A wolf might tear   result   I carefully undid
The visual   two-tones snapped reality back to
A safer and more mismanaged place so bungling

Dreams that even the most improbable leafy romp
Escaped with minor fury   as critics turned their
Heads like daylight which removed we had not got

And got on beautifully in arrears   as quoted us
Not half   a room for spectacular midnight error
With such big eyes   do they burn and they do

To leave rough edges dazzling down the middle
Where an unremitting moon tracks nothing right
Not time   and in a vacant lot I purchased well

A deviation in some doubt   in a looking-glass
Rewarding long teeth and a careful appetite more
Happily   through such insufficient pasts I wept

THIRD PARTIES

for carrying the can

Some disease this is   to be embarking on   machine
Readable in all particulars   life if you will to spare
In accelerated pale repose   the new downloaded run

To waste   waste words and tissue   not quite out
Of but rather into areas of fine control   to measure
Up the sometime weather   voices of the almost wild

One had better say easy at the prospect   yellow as
A sun unready even now to set   so someone handy
Is pointing it out   the missing adjectives the verbs

Of rise and fall   how a body becoming sure of itself
Knows naturally which way love turns   even more
Pure science please permit   rose compasses to reckon

The on-line mind   here grant spectacular licence as
A stranger — last indeed of the marvellous impossible
Introductions — makes the most sees nothing wrong

Rude health itself transmitted   or caused to crash
Grey waves   the long Atlantic happenings elsewhere
Ravishing   one letter out of shot to bemuse a day

REACHES AND BEYOND

The River Mole, *showing its friskiness chiefly by*
curving turns, or by cascades too neat to be natural

— A.R. Hope Moncrieff, *Surrey*

So   ever so much for that   rethinking not just
The ending   easier than I thought   but then
Who knows   red-faced the sum of the unnamed

Parts seen looking in   it's immaterial of course
The theory's still not up to it   putting its finger
On it   concretes?   no matter the aggregation

It's endless here at least with virtues of its own
And you can check direct   avoid the endless
Bother of exchanging lessons   go instead for

Madame de Staël's 'delicious sojourn'   in lumen
Loosely billowing out of harm's way   just
Abstainable from meaning what it won't   one

Object of the exercise unhappy   but only when
It's beating round a sullen bush   you can't say
That   and why   objections soon shot through

Like watered silk are patterned   informing me
Of their certainty   I can't help that   the first
Things fast no argument as a light pulls through

ON-SET INTIMATIONS

out of anaesthesia

I

Not a soul about   this time of night its gifted
terms and text that the state's agreed   non-urgent
with advances paid in kind   to whom does he divulge

a constant barracking of cloud   italics attached
to every other word   regardless

Lost rhythm and here's the sound of it   slow
turning keys   it seems self-questioning must do for
dialogue   now hope is entering into it   its 'regulation
rooms'   don't ever touch the lights

2

Full moon   decision making time   the work
towards 'stylistic difference'   *if*   you can find it
between belonging and owning   a figure and a landscape
note again the subtle management of 'distance'

off-stage cries and afterwords   a crafted pause
for whatever will do for inspiration

Maybe it's easy maybe it isn't   the seminal
essay is one that wraps itself in 'light'   impasto and
mud are of themselves   one world a gilded frame
for *form* read *field*   stake out as you must what's
'closely argued'   living life

3

It's another tactic is force   here in the
expression of *delight* and cannot help it   stop me and
listen   we're getting there now   your song   those
last surprise equations   call (recall) me back

quick installation (under cover of shadow) of
an engine-like contraption   the faintest of sounds
commitment   cranking up

Complete so savour it   not hard when it
won't let up   just listen to the hammering 'rain' whose
day it is   delight?   but I wouldn't hang around in it
and anyway the question is who's doing whom a favour?
quits

4

Do I believe in it   in red through rain   a
backdoor maple shaking out 'biography'?   and what
of truth   this jumping jack's November?   telling
and hard which re-remembered lights to die for

eruption of leaves and papers across stage
minor characters at sixes and sevens   'in hot pursuit'

The questions register   if only a spell in the
life of words   brief seasons   and maybe I've seen
them out for balance   my expectation's a still but
less than silent air   absolved   red talking up another
brilliant fall

5
Days when I got it wrong   occasions lost in
monochrome   blue light and not exactly reason gazing
out   there's cloud if nothing else to count   small
matters come (as illustrated) to a head   you'll find a
not uncomplicated distance

*small alterations only   a window opened and
door left ajar   a heavy coat (it's not clear whose) is
slung over the chair*

It has to be *now* ...   the words maintain a
quiet insistence   but whether or not they care?   the
sky's more difficult   it's said when programmed
absence treats itself to 'sign' ...   predict the shadow
these numbers gathering centre-stage

6
Phosphor and tinsel half the night and good to
be awake in it   it's Sirius keeps me playing up   mad
beacon   the calling steady as she goes   'don't go'
for ever time and again (dark waves) we're burning up

*reducing stage to a bleak exterior   rocks and
rubble   a breath of wind from nowhere   music and promise*

Crackling energy   amazed and why not be
awake to it   chorale the words we mean (don't
underestimate) this space   here's content   stars too
many more than you can shake a fist at   whispering
fits   and starts

MUTUAL REDESIGNATION

1 Forensics are working up to it   with luck
complete distraction leaves no trace   one death
and it's writing up the past   with gifts like love
and madness in arrears   but yes plain staging's
fine by me   I'll entertain enlightenment any time
brute clouds start billowing in the west   let the
blues demystify   I'm clueing my best work in

2 Serious as a lost midsummer can get   by
any other numen   there's lightning over lives
and a need to keep this brief   I'm here forgive
me medicated   out of it for appearances' sake
still sheltering under trees   by 'slender hopes'
I mean the missionary condition   safety first
and the goodtime balance held in trust

3 Some novelty this in store   some promise
it's a veritable end to waiting   for lights to
change   what better gift than sainthood   life
rebrand the herd?   but that's a world away and
the game is on   I'm venerating nothing till my
brief turns up   with an endless product range
anticipation struggles to up its stake   go green

4   Just ghosting through the past   redesig-
nating elders   a text of stunning imperfection
makes a life of Riley   all the facts got up in
glad rags for a song   don't breathe a word of
it   recrimination's bounty   when your ship
comes in see dislocation ready and able   long
nights safely in the bag   entrancing disrepair

5   Position yourself against the rest   watch
Autumn like no other   its plain conversion of
the past with meaning out in style   a conspic-
uous maybe pale remission   with sin reordered
seeing what sin became   guess what   a child
starts out   his shadows readmitted and ready
to burn   new colour raging flagrant as intent

6   Tonight and for one night only   welcome
this lying in state of angels   contraptions that
can't be faulted   thinking who is it dusted off
deceased?   as it all comes back   odd angles
never the one you guessed   no doubting guilt
by association   let's see one wing and a prayer
rephrasing chance   you bet this world's acute

7   It doesn't take much to retrieve the loss
madeover miracles pure gymnastics   but some-
thing to warm to   come what may   philosophy
happens   keeping its bravest smile till last   as
home fights off a shadow   checks misfortune's
putting itself at risk   who knows   which con-
tract's written to last   writes just returns

8   Why wait for reservations   there's a grace
to the taken line   biography believes me though
it's still forgotten in the rush   watch out   as
security purposes stake their uninvited claim
it's now or never   two guests at a table replete
with goodness   factual and luminous both while
hope debates new futures   beckons us in

9   Unplanning the next hiatus   why is it
no-one's told me the dark convertible's changing
lanes?   here nothing is slipping so neatly into
place   with dreams at record levels in retreat
I'd hoped to make my choices known   when
you're any and every place I'm lost good order
yawns   it's affection crashes   out of mind

10   Exaction   it's true things leave me help-
less   rueful   practising hard two-fingered runs
describing a lake as 'silver'   I'm out of bounds
I admit to the kind of joy you'd weep for   like
yesterday's hand-me-down now out of surgery
in stitches   remote and 'blue'   as a gift found
wanting   taking to heart unguessed refraction

11   Small wonder at least comes out of it   un-
menacing creation   for 'how it is' read 'maybe'
but primary?   history sees to its colours   its
tyrants   well disposed to words   like 'passion'
energy can't verify a thing   poor focus runs
the gauntlet with a will   the world's unmoved
try harder   unstacked books all balance out

12   Uncanny precision   the cloud and the para-
digm are making a clean descent   her brush of
words trails here-for-the-moment messages over
blue   greed's highlights   undergoing a rapid
but suitable restoration   she's here for the fear
with unrarified creation   no slouch is casual
making its mark in gold   whose lost works sell

13   More megabytes than the screen can deal
with   no-one out there knows me   rehearsing
crime   as the day comes warm and willing   a
slap in the face for futures   and their territorial
ambitions   clairvoyance is proving the last re-
liable witness   midnight glows with rank affec-
tion   I hear what might be crashing its gears

14   City to city   making some extra   who *is*
it   this stranger riding out a wave?   no it's not
strictly legal   if a well loved duff refrain   as
innocent as putting a dodgy deal on ice   so old
books give it   up for the prophet   handouts
never in decline   whose land is their land   an
unknown scintillating over water   pricing us out

15   At one remove or another   the exquisite
is proving hard to read   amazing say reductions
for every sidelong glance a one-way trip to con-
flagration   agreed I'm barely out of intensive
bruised   with hardly a simple word left standing
where I'm at   disease itself is something wicked
to behold   the funerary gets itself free-wrapped

16   So theory's got a green light ...   active
tracking those 'stormy waters' to an end   art's
small transparencies   and hopes   to declare
which wave slipped landward proves a word
... as 'silvery'   no matter   failing hard on
good ears   knows me better   a long beam in
the eye   and senses oceans   all found out

TO MIMICRY

Coppiced and coded   it may have mattered
Then   so wooded   but the shadows still
More thinking   and somehow you know it
Well enough   to do   this swirl of breezes

Cursive   troubled you might say   much
The same   same independent story   when
It's finished   and yes it's almost through
With telling me one and all   you're given

A lively dance or two   once over it's out
Unmattering beauty with a will   for what's
Sake caught up   gleaming in the stress of
Things   at large a dream is vulnerable too

In blossom   pure at the roadside mapping
It out   the syringa's whitefall   only love
To lay the word down   and harder is it?
Becoming   the sirens throbbing and calling

Up the usual distances   myself   now plain
And variable morning light   a moon hung
Over finds me a coffee to the good   with
Dazed heads at the casement 'ready ... to

Face it'   tribulation?   I'm strictly amazed
To have got this far   uncloudy whatever
The sky says   a new day's junket   just
As before and despite   'the music'   made

FLYING COMMENTARY

Back and forth   particular movements   same
As ever   they're giving nothing away   can
Anyone stand it   version 1 gives up the obvious
Arcane and wild meanderings ... version 2 is

In denial   but you see it something don't you
Like a needle   it's silvery and busy and rapidly
Pursued by vapour   as absorbed as they are
Themselves in the reading   not for the eye

To pick out   the heavy surpluses   of prosody
Of time out or a light that won't break down
These windows the walls and doors   anticipate
More slow corrosion in the works   real people

Move to that   they know what kind of rust's
Engaged   constructing a catalogue of ready-
To-alter states   don't disappear   do they say
We need you and what if specific pieces don't

Connect?   no matter   what the world thinks
Loving the circuits   the overlapping and in-
Determinacy seen now in the picture as vapour
All breaks up and disappears   more like it

Blue then   formless as the sirens sound   no
You couldn't make it up   not all the all-
Clear's history   here turning a chapter's end
In   grave as a cloud is   thief to the light

LOW ELEVATION

Never off-guard   ready to deal with the most
Extreme of situations love hears you   breathing
Half-guessing at what comes next   diffused
Through protective glass   unreal illumination

See   you make it up as you go   it's an issue
Kept to the forefront   instant to the thinking
Sacrificing words for even better words   like
Truth itself   arrived at   minus its clothes ...

Do you know your mind   the last thing on it?
Asks someone hovering   don't let duration in
All epigraphs attached can be viewed as foreign
You cannot pretend it's easy   before and after

Are taking an age to throw a light   know just
Where the exits are at all times   whoever it is
Distributes the gold   free-thinking   it's braver
Choices sense a conflagration   your orders

Demanding you switch the engine off   expose
A difficult nerve   the pain that gets you there
Pleads guilty to every charge in a scenery that's
Often redundant   letting the thought slide past

The last thing on my mind is thunder   a crush
Of colours that manifests itself in subtexts
Close by there's a drift of yellow lupins a river
To relate   unmeasured time   a broken bridge

YET TO BE: THE PERFORMANCE

And be ready for it   'a small world'   treasures
This meeting in all its finery   left unplanned
Not an awkward shadow falling   worth a look
Does this   new after-image meet with approval

When you see it   like now reflected   the small
Half-chances   a pedestrian in a street of willed
Delirium   lights concur   controlling a daze
Of mauve and massive purple spikes   one large

Rosette of gold   will such be enough to go on
Highlights set up for anything you see   worth
Noting   somewhere here's an interchange you
Could use   I recognise the glow   on the look

Out for love its extraordinary like   to measure
Tall dark trees responsive now sweeping a glitter
Down at the lake   demands in duplicate   walk
Here   be ready or not for order   as you turn

The coming day round   ready when something
Grips   slow-witted and brighter if unexplained
This major life you gather piece by piece toward
The obvious   best putting the words away I

Set all zeros to a finer tolerance   whose last
Odd-angled planes are taking centre-stage   to
Catch?   more haloes than the saints can   life
Running out of colours   do I remember which

LOVERS' LEAP: PART SONG

Classic fiction   of poetry and legend's
England   a dream out over the pond
Half-way ...   holds ghosts per million
Counting parts   pale midges a water

Drop could scatter but when or where
It's guessing   a light keeps shadow
Busy   and makes the best of company
Unknown   unpractised in the art of

Leaping   head back feet up into sky
There dizzy to keep a watchful eye on
Nothing   it's good no news is   even
The going my underfoot   accepting

Which plain life's abbreviated   a fair
Account of virtue   hanging on every
Word the rope pays out   undone
Oak's greeny-gold affair   left over-

Hanging   soon enough grubbed up
Put paid to   guilt?   remember well
I do like nothing else remember   so
The story goes   it licks its wounds

READJUSTMENT

Not having it   this or anything   read as
'Finished'   as seasonal fare   so it begins
And surely ends with the canvas dragging
Having the paint run   exhibitions ragged

Not stopping at the world   its increase
Wild   come any occasion not to measure
Change till a life's worked out   its colour
Making do with frames   plain clockwork

Grey   as figures go about their business
Not quite present   to a future left behind
It seems the viewer's looking on   if over-
Wound   some platform this   and worth

A gamble?   slowly now as things observe
Their cue re-reading the latest instruction
A half-step backwards   with maybe little
Said   and less removed   I'm sending up

Not one but two identities   well met here
Beyond the door   it's a green and glassy
Atrium and my picture's nothing   mobile
As the year is eloquent   keeping it sweet

VANTAGE POINTS

country roads

Walking away just brushing it off   seeing
What else might do   tomorrow will try
A different route   long branches I packed
With blossom for delight   more times of

Our lives laid down for somewhat premature
Recollection   spilt what passed per moment
To give myself away in choice disguise   it's
The final act   unnaturally before the first

And likely here I turned   respectfully into
The skid my world saw coming   is this
Acceptable?   not knowing the worst   but
A word in jest   storm-frenzy's someone

Else's job to handle   here in one layby or
Another under trees I'm looking up   which
Part is easy but this?   it can't be anywhere
The centre holds   if not the text   consult

Some other miracle   if nowhere words can
Quit the script   no need for spare parts
Everything is passing fair   a daydream of
The feint as petals still and leaves fall white

PROMISING ADVANCE

for the readings

This is the way to begin   sun low as it gets
Is putting its O on the line   not Summer not
Anything like it but the whole thing restless
Flowing   like real friends put the clock back

Information sizzles   with circuits out of joint
It's a liquid chapter   someone else's verse and
Starriest of modes   but this heart is English
Temperate and bit by bit in love   love gives

Its still unequalled damn   rhymes unequivocal
With till   times head abroad   the shady bower
That randomises all who enter   please don't
Interrupt   the conferents all go down unaided

Whirlpools to dislocute response   an amazing
Grace   however you put me down   for one
Who lives and breathes   informs on anything
That falls   more gravity's on tap   let's say

It's red for something   hanging fire   I don't
Believe I know the messages pretend it's nature
Daybreak tips us over   linear the left brain
Takes a right to mayhem   spells it   'flower'

MARKET LEADER

Loaded down with all the coloured parts
Of the deal   not luxuries but almost
The same this day as every day keeping
A tab on things   the hatchback drives us

Over the limit   winningly at the brink
Look down and I swear   undying sighs
It's a fine affair   displaces the meaning
Every time I turn a corner   Autumn's

Waiting ready to read me up with scant
Attention to the heart   snow falls to
Plan?   a terrace reviewing the massive
Clearance   should love take heed   will

You ever play this back   the skidmarks
Black   to the real who's waiting signally
In sight at the junction   seconds right
So what   if the verdict's in our favour

It's the last escape on offer our interests
Finally on the up   plain speaking glitters
Selfless in its glory   my how different
My sweet persuasion voting with her feet

CLOSE ASSOCIATES

> the Mole, varying *its mood between*
> *weedy shallows and curdling pools*
> — A.R. Hope Moncrieff, *Surrey*

The facts do agree on it   it's a better place
To walk   abstraction's in a class of its own
In Winter   the manner in which through
Dialectic the most unlikely word will freeze

Lives come apart or meander   merge more
Likely   with the flint-grey cloud he quotes
For a middle ground   bewares another wave
Of emotion takes reality on   glossy black

It's making it hard for special detail   kindly
Concerns   and no point pointing loneliness
Up   a long week's prearranged with cloisters
Bankside energy and adherence to the familiar

Faith   genius knows a fine work when it sees
It   slow-mo's checking us out   additions all
From within   the fantastic gable a ponderous
Wing to keep at least one generation airborne

Up and about   community finds us diffident
Hours to kill   take a note miss nothing fancy
Being with you   when its *stealthy course is*
Trapped *in private grounds?*   if you're game

WORKING FREQUENCY

the broad main thoroughfare

Wanting   it's to know it   intermittent as
A workman scraping out his mixer   rain
The sequence rushing its tyres through wet
How well today runs   running its book

Through the words and beyond   the blue
Considerable moment   more argument
What time d'you call this then   tomorrow
Tells me   and something fairly strict of

The changes   just lately it's the wayside
A wildflower opens   just a breath   I'm
What a small sigh means   assigned again
To a series watching the drops I cling to

Crash   and not for nothing   I'm out
With a world to give   reflective non-dark
Only   its drift and fancy up to my eyes
Redressed in habit   compelled you know

To countenance   what groundwork's ready
For bricking up   tomorrows steal away
And no shock love refigures   all my plans
Turn a bout of half-inched decent words

To fooling   days I reckon outdo the faery
Nothing notices   the engine   its stopping
And starting   didn't I hear the forecast?
A *flowery mead* a *melody*   scattered *time*

CABARET OF PARTS

Making it not making it up   because it really
Isn't there   it's just a matter of time   like
When you reach the third line   when the sun
Clouds over   it's better to go inside says one

Black square   seeing the lights come steadily
On   if only   everything could take enamel
Straight from the can   try getting an essence
Into consultation with the mind and balancing

The red and silver and yellow boxes   gather
Substance in the park   not a lonely sentence
Wanting more   or less   are the ones with
Pictures under their arms to know the way?

Nil speculation desperandum   nothing but feel
The weight of theory unpronounced   for
Truth try taking a short cut   where the roses
Go   under the wheels   the boxes revving up

While painterly ploys emerge undressed   as
Any king is   altogether counting the last two
Lines as one   who knows himself in touch
Belongs to no-one   make it free association

With the first unspoken thing in mind   a cry
Undoes the child   it's zero time and again to
Bow   in part to the last inevitable   nothing
Is full of hope   strange weathers make it new

CLOSING TITLES

for an idyll

June   is it some other kind of rhetoric
Makes it   now the least forgotten sky
Shades into movement   like the blossom
Of a few poor words for bruising   finally

And all too generously in hock to love
Left over from some time you'd think of
Plenty   oh but just the most remarkable
Of storms   I'm readying again to move

Daylong and patient at the prospect   light
Feinting   never the first to leave   its gold
And first intentions pave the way for calm
Or   do they take the breath away?   dumb

Signalling only need   as foreign particles
Drift their pale particular nothing on the air
Check *no admittance* to a ghost   it's down
To ancient calculations?   darkening here

Like thunder in the wings   who's mixing
Things up   cannot put a name to it   so
What   if any close or distant heart
Picks up this faint vibration of another

Knowing   what will not be known   days
Better light than never   alchemilla   flower
Of the moment blowing   up for any
And every jilted dream words call to arms

FAITH AND VALEDICTION

AS IN LIFE SO BEYOND

1

Film   as a certain world goes by?
Haranguing   it's a sheen remembers

Asks no questions but tilts one eye
To 'murder'?   fanciful white words

Say something   say the first thing
In your head   a 'bullet'   who knows

Why ...   the handkerchief is folded
Round a gleam   no dream disclosed

To motive   frame by frame suspicion
That I might know its name suspects

2

It was afternoon   two yellow birds
And Summer dancing in its hollow

Searching clarity   not that the girl
Was hiding   or cared for formulae

Life's smooth unusable repeats   to
Play with ...   a mean kaleidoscope

Clouds distant   whispering no   no
I don't recall that shadow leaving

A line on substance x and y my
Something and nothing run to ground

3
No character is seen to disagree   it's
'Neutral emptiness'   as much by night

As word of mouth   yet nothing's more
Alive on-stage than colour   with detail

Harrying a mind   love's good if grave
And tender dreams aren't thinking how

To deal with stars   immodest and up
To no good   reason itself's entrapped

In matter   tone by tone fetched down
Delight ...   love's darker working out

4
April   here's a queen wasp looking
For a home   transition and revelation

It's undercover art   not easy as
Someone's life goes down to express

Relief   'black stripe on a hard black
Field'   it's abstract and it's essence

True to form and still to come   long
Summer straight from the tube   if

Minimal   all's zinging   tones in tune
Who can't see how to make it home?

LOSING MARKERS (5 a.m.)

There's a world and not a world   and anyone
Here   consider   I'm disabused of difference
Unseen costs incurred are ready to speak up
Only yesterdays working on it   when a coastal
Fog rolled up   all colours making one   divide
Only stave off please the inevitable   execution

It's an art   when a curlew calls out answers
There's work to do in conversation   listen in
To the finer frequencies   metaphor I wouldn't
Mention   the blue and white vessels all lined
Up for knowing   I'm overstocked and overdue
More rarified excursions as love goes begging

The question   is it the miracle's still tied up
What else?   can't always speak of blessing
Still it's the palest grey   still waters and a sky
Remembered   turning a murky red till nothing
But beauty burned   estrangement is definitely
A word I'm tracked by   when the light goes

Well provisioned in its other and handsome art
'Escapes' ...   sets my foreign histories loose in
Natural red   those traditional cotton covers
Glazed for discovery   don't tell the teacher
But hand me them all my hand-me-downs   if
You're passing take me for a sign and granted

A word is putting the times to shame   dawn
Raiding hordes   do I not forget them   cause
A wind to blow   soon clearing   maybe even
The least respected distances ...   do nothing
Till the colours glow   drop charges   anchor
Changes ...   certainly   I do for a price undo

EXHIBITION

the fixtures and fittings

Autumn   into the museum the impossible's
Easier now to adjust   whatever happens will
Provide our present space   negotiate or die
There's not a culture left without   re-read
The index   if you're openness itself   a sky
Of exquisite pictures has children singing or

Tearing headlong down a field   or crushed
As one was under boulders   did I tell you
The trees were felled how machines start up
With maps to accommodate a taste in true
Relief   some old estate and everything must
Go   rephotographed to run down contours

Light surveys   and a heron lifts in disbelief
At the clockwork word   its code and date
Unfree to improvise or fall   the leaves are
Settled in their mantras long since   'money
And quantity' described an arc that's turning
Heads   stack shelves and practise the means

Of ultimate production   there's something
Too heavenly attracted here   whose offer's
Over where creation signs ...   blue signals?
No you can't subscribe   less view it   it's
The best case ever   low sunlight emptying
Files in confidence   never to quit this space

PROSPECT AND VACATION

On time   and curious if I weren't still shuffling
Down the queue   more letters stamped for later
Winging out away   mute madness   to fit you
Yet for nothing   but?   the eternal greenback
A seaview   the almost empty car park   long
Stay I shall dedicate to no-one   no-one knows

The price   whatever's in store   and fundamental
In its stream of faded bunting   do I recognise
The tradename?   is this the ever-present witness
Of the world misplaced?   don't ask the question
Gulls don't overstay their welcome   with a scream
The daft allusion dresses up in white   the more

Anonymous the more the grey I'm used to   to
The fore   long curving out and down   down to
The conscious   dazzle if you will   anarchic words
Not first nor lost times   choruses hard sung
That leave me short   mistreat no other exile
So   who works like crazy   for any and every

Dark consideration   odd it's a child makes clear
The choice on offer   no-one knows   what's grist
To someone's mill   it seems   too tempting now
To say   it's tragic   every black-framed copy
Shows a form that's empty   random as the next
Horizon   light like murder   due again in kind

SUPERIOR WISDOM

Spectral   in the way that nationhood's
Latterly playing the field   but sounds
No not a bit like thunder   more cloud
For a bright eye narrowing the tale   I
Take your word for it   it's only later
I don't quite recognise the tune   much

As I want to   fading now   lost haloes
Are cleared for handing back   you call
More carefully the relevant number   as
Requested?   the frontier's closed   and
There's counting heads   like worlds be-
Yond   for why   to let unreal eventful

Drama in   weird and eco-frightful as it
Gets to many a folk come down with it
Best Offers   your choices gift-wrapped
Making a meal of wintry words   like
Love   *Can you do without it?*   taking
A frozen hand   my mind appropriately

Dressed   this is just believe me another
Stop-gap   a bleached out knotty fence
My thoughts couldn't turn to   better
By far though that we jumped at it and
Met the language halfway   hailing your
Stateliness undone   for our darkest act

PREDETERMINATION (INDOORS)

It is still   several clear blue layers of what's
By now no question a beautiful day   and may
Be longer   only time?   for the bickering of
Sparrows   unseen   though trying as I might
The numbers won't come up   you bet   to
Considerable amusement ... more party piece

Than nightmare he said   knowing it wouldn't
Do to ravish change   much less consult a few
White clouds   obscure?   I'll keep the more
Unlikely if delicious colours down   an ugly
Rumour making the singular reminder needed
Please be   it's both of us awake and fancying

The tilting of an unreal world   at windmills?
No swerving eye and never vindictive   black
Murder   for the book he's reading (a typo's
Dreading) gets the wind and someone's dander
Up   to meet ourselves in miniature   light's
Ready   to turn the clock back   play it again

STREET CREDIT

What once we were   well there were many
And not so subtle   continuous warnings
We are not quite right for   fashion   its
Verve and satin   strictly running away with
Us   astounding the sleek   fired up they're
Ready to be so coloured   to be equal to it

Seasons perpetrate a better class of crime
Taking nothing   not even the social element
Into any account of hope   it's dress again
Like crazy   there's no tomorrow an apricot
Moon's half out of cloud and falling   strictly
Cash   no worries   it's the price of a look

Looks sideways into camera   sends a hint
Of darkness   assures I'm the only mystery
There is and grateful   so ridiculously plain
It's almost graceful   as could be supposed
A consideration though it's just the thought
Of it starts here   red flashings probably fit

REFERENCES FOR NOVEMBER

Is it here   the explanation's not detectable
The sky you voted for now filling   while
A brushstroke waits impatiently for the nod
I ask what's left what's not go easy on us
Almost out of their way to please   a treat
When the big wind blows   you accept it

In the key of your choice as intensity may
Not   grow deeper than a blush?   there's
Still the warning   connections   to leave
A light on some think permanently   every
Thing at risk and all I stand for   when
The alert's up-graded   caught in the rush

To quit   I'm the last to feel the weather
Banking on change in time and place   my
Record's next on the line   big pictures
Showing but who'll be in when I call   on
Interim resources   leaves falling gracefully
To keep their word   in designated fields

RESTORATION BY DEGREE

1   *Temporary shelters*

It could be any cathedral city   her visiting
and delighting   lost in the first and last hours
here   to think of nothing   but the 'trail' its
shadows' long irregular revelation?   her work
this wondering   how to make it out   the
best way often curiously refined   quick colour
sequences she's loathe to plan   or code

Recording the 'miracle'   believe in its form
its hopes   with little about to happen and less
to give   revise all thinking   contemplate her
landscapes   their detailed cold   'surprise' the
better word perhaps   an escape worth having
remember?   the flags their decent fluttering
love wearying over impossible ancient deeds

Impetuous formulation   but why the haste
a day in the life of distance?   proving sunny
enough   at least for the most part   travelling
solo armed with memory   but never the thing
some pretty picture maybe two for company
the ultimate in mind?   again exposing chance
to risk   she registers the long familiar rhyme

Glissades   and everything upcoming   some
new experience to toy with   don't tell me
her heart's in tune   she knows it   off already
investigating   the next best dislocation
yesterday's fatality on ice   today a fire on the
hill   she'll not be thinking twice or grieving
it's out and back   coincidence in joy takes two

2 *Ongoing maintenance*

I can't help finding it   deep in the work
she struggles with   even now this stretch of
'greenwood' driving back the storm   odd
futures   and matter of fact   they're seldom
devious   the way she wanted it   the calm
outside herself   removed   a stream of cold
wind coming on wisdom gasping   unawares

Like no-one else's   the hunger barely
out of keeping with innocence   these fancy
greens and golds   excuses   like lichen and
moss   new runes to satisfy the sceptic   in
execution rapid   whoever's counting the
moments   no-one now's appropriating light
which light she reckoned to give a face to

Walls obliterated   and wayside leaves torn
free   her palette's questioning   observing the
patterns of abuse   long histories of absence
but ... is she daring to frame the scene?   to
respond in kind?   the evidence mounts in
strict if wishful thinking   true as her word
and in its fullness a season turns to ash

Can anyone imagine it   the pressure?   the
work in lieu — long hours for sure — and
commensurate?   I'm moved to put a word in
for penance a fitful sleep   her fingers hover
poised to draw the line   conceive the moment
as a line of flaking heads all saints look down
and scoff   from which comes murder

3   Open structures

It matters   there's something to take away
from here   a shadow composing   life as lived
retaliates with a loaded brush   low arches and
overhanging cloud   she suffers   the small talk
making for high philosophy   half-made   when
walls give way   forget the mechanism the eerie
presence   her reds run crazy   out of true

A reasonable assumption   flawless execution
surely ...   the wind's attracted to its height
a colossus   a one-day gleaming   shaking out
what's loose   no book of hours yet found to
comment on her trial   faith's less than eager
and master masons know it   putting it to the
test   love's lost perspective

Materials flake   and yesterday forgets
itself   as explanation tilts her dream   I sense
a touch of absolution   self and anything she's
party to ...   relief   for courtyards cool with
rain   at last it's play she's re-inventing   now
some new economy of means   each image put
to arranging reconciliation   pacts

Would any lens admit   geography by right
for restoration   gestures she hoped to count
across a massive range of frequencies?   taking
by halves instead to decorated margins   what
else?   an ancient mariner a dolphin pointing out
the way   light smears and smudges   her
minor charts to fix   and heaven itself to pay

PROSPECTING MIRRORS

1
Face values as received are making make-believe
the slightest area of sky is multi-layered   myth
comes chrome and coloured as a gift   its four
wheels leaving the road for dead   you know for
loving me read loving them   is this the song I
can't shake off?   dull interests are laying claim
to waste   for what it's worth   velocity is all
the rage   off-loading light for nothing   oh my
word it's not the dark streets underwrite escape

2
Fast running out of cloud   I'm ready for sense
and worse   for less specific dreaming   much
like kindergarten now as then   the atmosphere's
uncoloured and pre-ordained   returns to gravity
the simple silvering of minnows   note   my
instant disappearing   act of the first held frog
to jump   my misquote surely   life's the better
half of dream   what shock is there like waking?
breaking   the same and different world in two

3
To the one unsound proposition add another
continuous mad creation   here in my history of
hope I sometimes think it didn't happen   horrors
it did   new colour programmes faked the longed
for smile   perspectives catching tenderness in
tow   less abstract now as the days go by more
private   home is the last invention   flowers fill
every room   imagine a study underlit by stars
by arrangement   an angel to spread its wings

4

Closeness   this and everything worth working
on   under fire   by firesides hand to hand
efficiencies achieved   nights blessed with simple
recognition   better I'm told to keep the rest of
it under lock and key   especially now with the
word out closing deals   her claim she'd once
seen Eros 'flying' ...   which going by the book
proved hard   not that she'd place a bet on it
love's fanciful weather   and safety coming first

5

Sunflowers and mercury   climbing higher and
falling out between the words   if only I'd got
away   not warmer climes but a half-day enter-
tained without a cloud   old friends to bargain
with in a present unsubscribed to loss   take
this on trust   love's moment even as it burns
today my well-thumbed pages take the world
on   at its own game   chance is as good as it
ever gets   blue brochures seeing off the light

6

Friend   friend in a hurry make it happen   as
maybe the powers will not   subdue   or be
subdued   we're still at the checkout   smiling
grave goods in their golden true proportion all
stack up   belief?   it's a total education   get
some fresh air   in a word be true to form
the gift is in repair   who knows the half of it
when all day's lost account is found in balance
heaven send   the index knows its own

RUDIMENTS OF HAPHAZARD

when one war is over

It is surely a familiar glance of hers   undone
Amazement   making the best of a bad job
She would mention the big black racketing clock
Or the drawing room turning its face to dust
That deviate   not for a minute   to a point

In the middle distance   its long cascade of
Steps   do you see she eyes it all   a scene
That shivers   as the blowzy crowd moves in
With stethoscopes and medallions several piles
Of coins   a deliberate scattering of things

In black and silver which she knows as hers
Pale butterflies clinging flaking to the cornice
Such unbridled muchness   access easy enough
To guilt   to unspeakable solace   a face that
Now she thinks of it is quite ungracious   still

To write   her saving lines and sweet mistake
Words   with their riddle   however she thinks
Them   often minus the past that dreams itself
Admiringly into ornate mirrors   if she wakes
And thinks   the future now's with half a mind

Elsewhere   in longhand   terraces are active
Taking the air   more thoughts   she's making
Do with   Sundays   just her lyrical isolation
And nothing in it   for the rhododendrons or
The half-built summerhouse   as imaginative as

The hand may be   delight is all too obviously
Less than gilded   the centrepiece of another
World   rehearsing rather less than diligently
The consequences of her age   not one word
Has it confidently   a bad job merely bettered

HARD GROUND

and full

It was a crowded history   in basic terms the facts
Were fewer than people   competition inspired more
Alternatives than a page could hold   I was keen
To be there till I saw the tide was still coming in
The red skies turning real   considering it was mine

For nothing   choice wanted only to ask about
Yesterday   the appearances the sound of decisions
Never taken   who now spoke substantially costing
The trouble   when if only I'd been there mindful
About changing course   just recognised the signs

What then?   the wild and the unspecific the truly
Unspeakable   a perfect eradication   but fill in the
Blanks   get events no matter how ghostly to mat-
Erialise   find that somewhere and someone 'neither
Logicious nor musicious' as a wicked wit had put it

'He'd keep his best foot tacet on the ground'   so
Letting the absent eye light up?   a future ready to
Be dated   not now   the names put to all the life-
Size reproductions everywhere on show   you know
I woke up too many times last night for this to be

Other than natural   that old familiar plowman on
The cover   the dingiest olive you'll ever see   for
Every unillustrated face undoing the words inside
A furrow   it was night as we knew it   at a price
I respect   melodious folk song worth looking up

SHIFTING, TENSE

Wakings and costings   and which way out
No telling the rest   if it's still to come
The causes of it   family   stirred-up
A likely kid   and his puddle   but when?
Sun sweating   there's a cold haze into

Hard belief   may I   believe this Mendips
Morning present and correct   a three-note
Crow for shadow?   I'm off downhill on
A one-gear bike tyres grumbling   hear
That farmgirl blue-eyed saying her be for is

Which counts?   if taut and logical   like
Bluebells   spiking a half-remembered mist
It's just statistics   a resurrection almost
Five decades   with maps and a catechism
Blushes for governments   changing office

Oh the smile of it   this April of Other
Still justifying how it was   and never
Never over the muddle   the sweet track
Out   so what I'm back   still not at odds
With thinking   the milk is thick un-

Pasteurised   live colours intermittent
And stations more than hard to get   wait
On   they'll tune themselves in   surely
Past psychology and daybreak?   ice on
The water   more splashing and waking up

Field Trip, Rodney Stoke, c.1955

SELF-EVIDENCE AND SUCH

for the archive

Asking   is this exact?   a copy of
The prayer   reduced to the sound
Of background information   light
Steeped in a milder fixative   even
Addicted   but not to another name

Whose colours're loved by morning
Seeing the finished portrait leave
To breathe   choose 'matters of fact'
This world then   hardly   she said
Diminishing   and unknown almost

Blessed by distance   no topography
No memory   or none she'd want
Revealed   so much for questions
The situation calls if ever it does for
Me   I'm here   and waiting really

Only a sentence stopping at nothing?
The message   acquired with practice
Conditional in the way it's wanted
For a chamber barely lit   how well
She'll pretend   the story   thus far

Reading tolerably okay   'true life'
The omnipresent job that's guarded
Elsewhere   given or taking a pause
To dream   an instrument of belief
I cheer credulity in lonely draughts

EVERYMAN

Castles   to break the hold of virtuosity
Stripped   a black field thinking of where
I'd been when majesty do you remember
The story too many clouds rode by   I
Have to say it finished and finished well

A flat land indulged in scribble   west of
The river its huge barns ready for almost
Anything   wind-blown futures the price
In freefall no-one now's prepared to read
Mythology into it   which who's the lost

Prince hiding out in grandeur who knows
They're seeing to it   reducing the point
Size going for subtler proportions stories
Overlooked like a hedgerow   by some
Errant saving knight and in the reckoning

Returned to self   almighty shudderings
A costly halt as in days gone by a project
Not for nothing rears   in large-scale
Uninflected grids where brush and even
A nervous world expose us   to material

Limitation?   I witnessed them   I declare
I knew them well   accelerating smartly
Into the 'last unknown'   no don't try me
Out   my signs for places when the mind
Turns up in colours   take a neutral field

PAINSTAKEN

for clarity and for respect

Establishing an orchard   your bearings   hard
By a culture disestablished   it's a day's work
And then some rhetoric committed to the cold
If not yet frozen   themes out and picking up
The pieces   the sweet and sour their basketful

For whom it's right   the question ever   am I
The one to ask prepared   to look I look   is
That enough   what else can only be imagined
I'm not a palimpsest   expecting concentration
To squeeze out sensibility to break some other

Distance in   settling only for one thing   my
Place of deepness where a good thing falls   in
Love and war   it's the same sun   its slanting
Whenever you want it   in a landscape more
Cut out for argument   refine what's obvious

In a work of silence   one voice that'll cancel
Any other   a time to shine like plenty slender
As a branch is   branching   lifts amazement
To and from the archive   you reckon a word?
No   less the right word something more ideal

RECURRING BLIGHT

and rattling preconceptions

That combination of the planet's less plausible
Skills   redrafted through generations   to
Scarify his one performance   simultaneously
It's out-of-print and a lasting accomplishment
I move   over and above any possible slight

Meaning   stigmata from a bruised decade or
Two   still heaves in the Atlantic's improvised
Divide   to seem unmistakable   evolutionary
And shining   whatever conceptual aches remain
There's a newfound dialogue   rugged and real

Upheavals quick to the point of syntax   part
Steeped in another long-range forecast   open
To proof   so okay   a little lyrical constraint
Is imaged there   light blazing in the gnostic
A smooth transition   eye only for the random

Forms of truth in kind   it's the cosmologic
Handful handles thought to suit   translation?
More a summing up of loss   that readymades
Can worry   acknowledge how things are in
Words   heart's ritual moments fired to fade

AFFIDAVIT

and brute finds

A fable spreading fast   an authority speaks
Confident of fortune   and prediction grows
To levels never seen   such wonders   of
Decomposition   all the better to write this
Asking   truly is the skeleton intact   does

A record yet survive   unvisited in a foreign
State   unrecognised to its own?   some
Being there by contrast in its former — still
As I think it — perfect state shown fit   to
Sleep with madness?   contrive compassion

Thinking all we are   the world no stranger
Being   to satisfy our loss gales engineer
The shipwreck   often darkness palls against
Reflection   I'd rather the plot inhabit greater
Care   if knowledge paints in softer colours

Light can ravish   no sea-green superstition
Disenchants   here every twist and turn adds
Graver dazzle   beauty will ache to manifest
Imagine nothing   I measure only the least
Of last accounts   to be sure   beasts roam

Ex "Wonders of the Deep" by M. Schele de Vere

INTELLIGENCE

for the war game

Three parts invention when a dice lands
Hard on one edge toppling   some artist
For the day   you can hear him now re-
Act   inhabit is it worth it the altogether
Distant words and syntax   well why not

Amounts to the same thing   deadlines
Surely to relate the individual did I hear
Me say hard truth?   more detonations
In a nightsky black or white as atrocity
Fancies   the daisy's cutting it   heaven

Help   rescreen not really not again   he
Has your word for it   appalling smoke
Throws a double six but nothing yet you
Ain't   scene changes by the hour   and
Tongue-tied often   there's some fiction

Or other warring   so he says   a third
Time 'lucky break' though nothing comes
Of it   he's up as ever glassy-eyed and
Balancing the line   another world game
On   the rules engaging chance redrawn

HIGH WATERMARKS

Wild garlic   violets by the path   don't think
Of the voices   impossible research conducted
Into being   things grow together   a sacrifice
If needed when a storm blows in   some days
I'll slow it up   take a chance too many when

I vote by proxy for the winning hand   be it
Silence after rain   a numen or two   with
Flashing lights down a path to part-time glory
Usually it's friends of mine I visualize   so
Distinctly plotted   I imagine the least familiar

Flowers are turning in their brave (hear this)
Redoubt   a harmony of heads inclined the way
I see it to what comes raucous and maybe next
A page of jackdaws heaven has pre-selected
Unerring to this dark exaggerated place below

If minus the relevant components   everything
That glitters is a world away   not getting us
Nearly into shape   blue hyacinths cape daisies
So many wide-eyed escapees   only too happy
To go along with things   to misread the wild

PROSECUTING TRADE

... a Dane, who came on board the commander's ship,
having occasion to express his business in writing, found
the pen blunt; and, holding it up, sarcastically said: "If
your guns are not better pointed than your pens, you will
make little impression on Copenhagen!"
— Robert Southey, *The Life of Nelson*

It was how the day went   somewhere between
Marshalling the fates   and enduring monuments

Couplets   marrying spirit with a dash of fame
Pervasive as the scent is   mortal men decline

I will remain he said in humble admiration   only
The picturesque disquiets   draws process out

*

To be   an instance of continuous narrative one
Needs to dream   of touching   genius and death

But two alternatives   to quit the current order
Diligence here advances   forgetting what's next

He's seizing fancy   this is permanent worth   to
Chance on romance   cut and re-direct your fire

*

The semblance only of remission   he drank to
Sleep   a nod to inspiration   then louder grief

Classic disrespect   an age now past   considered
Prophecy the instrument of taste   I *will* be told

Nothing quite like it   a region once again laid
Bare   more youthful daring   joys up in arms

*

Appoint no monsters   the capital's already smoke
And fire   you'll labour afterthought with fangs

A minor occurrence   two distances in mind to
Discover politics is looking this way   only that

Scarcely inferior   their vessel boasted weather
As its generous next of kin   a shared account

*

LOCAL ABANDON

In the Middle Ages and afterwards paper making was
an industry inevitably associated with heresy.
— Arthur Guirdham

Out of a hundred walls   valerian   here's looking
To the ideal interval   getting things done   in time
Perhaps   no gospel like a welcome light   as if
New watchers prayed for it   where *now*'s another

World   and might be self-sufficient   in one guise
Or another   *never* gets a hold   who seeks a care-
Free licence likes odd moments to abstain   whatever
Is blowing in   it's the sea unchanging   revels in

Indisputable excess   comes such a day   as I do
Admire   that durable alliance   faith and valediction
But make me a picture of it someone   someone's
In it   like evaporating chance or fancy non-escaping

Fact   vivacious   as an unplanned garden tells it
A breath that's shrewdly chosen   soft   referring
The pink and red to a thousand blooms   life's glow
Non-native   or open to handmade dark?   revised

PARTICLE ATTRACTION

Guillelme was obviously practising the austerities
necessary in a Parfaite
— Arthur Guirdham

Raising mayhem   meaning   to pay for it
A little later   love tries out its book of
Small hours   hoping that resignation's
Running scared   finds sacred in the same

Few days gone by   supposing nothing
But cloud is uppermost in mind   a cold
Effusion   like concentration?   lights
Under water   other random base effects

To cloud a near resourceful eye   best
Pick my way again through meetings and
Partings   leave chance to flicker through
Acceptance   knowing the word is merely

Halflight   just the one trap set   and i.e.
You   play dead   no victim in the jaws
Of logic/atmospherics?   they won't detain
Unlikely narrative   a heart pulls through

HIGH READING

Still   many a smoky April morning   to back me
With a will   no thought what frequency's engaged
I'll buy it   taking the voice as birthright   time
Called in like favours briskly   betting on half

A chance with light out over cold ground   upping
Its stake to wings   to register an entry   tilt
The greater scheme of things this way   surprised?
You'd think   this day and age two minds are safe

Abroad   to conjure up well anything   a word
Wants? 'fairest delight'   as a cloud stop-starts
Can't settle   my one fixed sentence more than half
A deal   with trust extending through the thick

Of it   the texture of a thousand unknown moves
Like nothing do we say on earth   prime movers
At the making   never a meal of things by heart
Just listen   how the numbering of names is done

ORIENTATION

locate locate

Like they say   it's a limited distraction   playing
To the dark's a sign of the times   so   watch it
Watch over it you might say   flitting to and fro
About the orchard   do you hear the bat squeak?

These few words   recovering veering to the edge
Of Winter hard by the shadows   crystal sometime
White with thoughts   they don't appear   to what?
When the future's stacking up   half-hearted 'facts'

Don't get it   is how it all ends up   to have me
Double-cross the story   listen   it's many an hour
I'm meaning   whatever you think   and it could
Be this?   I worry   plot the unexpected distance

Quiet corners   try to mark them out for good
Till it's gone eleven ...   not that I've been here
Long   with a hush some character of yours might
Die for   squeak squeak   meaning nothing moves

UNSCENE HURTS

observing by absence

Longing to re-experience the unfamiliar past
And re-tune it   to less innocent present day
Conditions   you wouldn't dream of?   if
The papers weren't so decoratively achieved

I'd be getting it down to a modest proposal
The kind a council has a personal interest in
Opts out   as memory is stable so the heart
Conducts a perfect autopsy   laying out even

Broader ecstasies on the slab   as palimpsest
Sun-spangled pages   write nothing off   but
Lies   mysterious economies of desire   I'm
Game for madness if it comes to it   any old

Barge pole touching up the world   to excuse
A glade of euphemisms and thicket of night
I'll not come this way yet again   and passed
Best compliments to all   you'll know it well

CLOSE DISORDER

Sanctuary Wood 1915

Tornado on the south coast   the way
One picture narrowed   green to grey
And back   *and I remember* ...   more
Of how his 'orders' went   still making

Waves   genetic overtures   or something
Random wordless in the blood lights up
This dawn   the past historic   days can't
On their own renumber   flesh   to make

My way leaves down through trenches
Flooded   a fill of questions   oh
Quotidian stuff as last night's kills come
Begging   not for meaning not the letter

That's standard for the law   but breath
A place   to witness under slanting sun
At least this one pale spectrum   easier
To go for sure than come through storm

FOR SIGHTING

North Cornwall 1958

Stone walls   yellow flowers   a drop
No ledge   and nothing in particular
A history   that's writing I think it's
Writing the whole thing safely in and

Gladly   a cliff of detail   people will
Gather as they do look up astonished
So much and never so much   as now
The heart at such a distance trembles

Thoughtful ready to skip a beat   at
Being found with presence   birdsong
And light for composition unnecessary
Meaning   this is not theology   but

Movement   as in falling   the limits
Everywhere at hand a little anguish
Speaks perceptively of how I am in
Recollection daring a space to breathe

NON-EXPLANATION

in August

No pretending   no counterfeit notation   and
Not yet finished   amazed the lyric can slip so
Comfortably into a measure of deadly Summer
Shade   all promises scattered as I hear them

Scream   a reaction?   something reeking of
The long lost wild   the ordinary's better still
It lurks in the unused room   with flowers
More motives to imagine   suchlike boxes of

Delight you're quick to read though it's hard
To breathe   'forgive me the time is wrong'
Again?   I can't believe she says so   never
A memory only expectation   vanishing years

I'll try to see through   to effect some kind
Of illusion   on lips a consummation   to put
By words   the word goodbye is waiting for
Time   some cadence better equipped to burn

FOR THE STORY: AS THEY COMMITTED IT

England/Belgium 1915

Steering by now a haphazard course   out into
Further lapses   of green and recovered time

Much as she'd thought some future composition
Paying respects   here ostinato   the trembling
How a string of dreams might sound out chance
A first time   her lifetimes' shadows   breaking
Even at the last   she smiled at failure   words
Forever ready to leapfrog moments   catching
A misremembered brilliance   the eyes discursive
Only the hardiest flower and thorn knew how
With narrative now reading suntrap   narrow
Slices of light   what's said is said for the end-
Less asking of it   however gross in small print

Finding such work exhausting   her piece work
Looking up points of rest ...   gold lichen even

So she'll have to tell me   why those questions
Won't exactly answer ...   to the eerie precision
Brought to bear   on scope on possibilities for
Future reference   he last remembered making
For the front   shells falling   hardly of a mind
To dwell   mixed colours then as now congealed
According to the day   cross-threaded a melody
Bloody enough   he leaves the page transfixed?
Things calling out   so much the worse   would
They ever know   unwilling and willing histories
Undone his seeing variously complete   excused

Her occupation then unknown his fate surpassed
Since childhood what had happened surely would

PERADVENTURE

Bare boards for the most part   furniture

In store   the woodlice are making the most
Of easy come and   by the time this light
Is needed   go   quick miniatures   of ...
Composition   the easy breaks short-ordered
However they come   untried and devious?
To make themselves and all things scarce

If inspirational   a witness   guesses granted
Via a page of glass unframed   light riddles
My halfway house with tenderness and grief
What's creeping in and out of fact is distance
Heaven knows and I won't believe it   words
Dear nature cram your spreadsheet   do me

How you will   and never mind   the nicks
Fixed hieroglyphs are turning every shadow
Out of old estates   tree-fringed now dark
As the moment   making it hard   by folly
By starlit ornamental pond   the dogs sniff
Nothing out   exquisite prints they're frantic

Off cross-country as the word is   patched
To mend   it's a bosky text whose storm-
Fed rills I gamble on   hope's bender bare
And a habit doing the meanest favour   why
Not take it   so be over the worst   excess
Love's last attention sketched by dawn   a

Ring-fenced future   bramble & climbing rose

REFLECTIVE SKY

and its reckoned aftermath

Putting the word down   here's a palette

'July with Swifts'   and the numbers fewer
It seems continue to make a point   flash
There again … it's dark   the systematic
Know-how of remembering   that curious
And suspect centre-piece of storm   its
Irregular detail running from it   thought

A landscape   you saw to that?   not yet
Removed from terror and all its high-keyed
Drills   still handsome in the major mode
Though fraying   a nimbus for every cloud
Stacked up   it was business-like in truth
And you were quite exceptional   witness

The cool deliberation settled in the record
Things taped in black and white   for just
A minor screeching   pale a bit off-centre
And the crux by any other name   as swift
The curve of a perfect ellipse — tighter
So menacing   a word too strong perhaps

The same old story   now late and catching
A hill that fades in a fading light   it's yes-
Terday if you struggle gets it   the better
Cloud   more edge to edge reprocessing of
Hurt   the numerous small effects that fly
More freely you might say   quick figures

Of life   and death   in sumptuous accord

TIMEPIECE: THE ENGRAVING

Come back to this the waiting   flashlights

Down a long hour searching and windows
Owning up to nothing   the record here
Exaggerates the slightest movement   now
You see it and now you don't   the house
Stands by   back then it turned to silver

Brief enough   initials witnessing a name
Remade   it happens   whenever the need's
To have things gleam ...   'Remember Me'
It said   still says while leaves turn over
Slow   some other life   longstanding elms

I'd wonder at   no shelter   but reminder
Nothing's easy is it   absolution?   it only
Winds you up the more   with questions
Seeing   another drift come Autumn crisp
Well measured making up its mind   to

Put the last requested words to use   of
Course   you recognised the provenance
Guessing   what any return might prove
Dark histories dared you out   remember
The face the fact of it erratic   halfway

Luminous   a focus always prone to fade

PRECIPITATE

The drop I have to wonder at   syllabic cell

And see-through memory I thought was fixed
With every expedition   soon undone   found
Ill-equipped   to change direction   willingly
I turn to something else   but short again on
Confidence make swift referral back to base

It's no surprise   the thing there's underlined
In red   more sources to research than any Nile
And checked for ...   if not found passed over
Silently till crazy   but when approved then
Every 'go ahead' turns sharply   into vertical
Invisible acceleration   and good times set

With paradigms in profit   look philosophy's
To hand   as much as I like to think it working
Out   it's hard back home   this rain   who-
Ever I am to see it now   who some indeed
Make plural!   some amusement   so here's to
Keeping busy   as business gets   with story

Rifling custom   a green light's simple nothing
To declare itself   on course   and all returns
In kind made clear   no 'facts' unfit to print
What futures   hearts in mouths   leave history
Small slippage   nothing more evident now

Than this   divided light   we have to fall

DRY SPELL (IN ITALICS)

Landscape jaundiced ...   certain grasses bending

To us the most elaborate   and close inspection
Of a world we knew   our backpacks overloaded
Green?   we'd strayed too far from home   too
Independent for our or anyone's good   removed

By Winter   brilliant crystalline   and challenging
That text   its lordly ash and aspen working
Over an ever-changing state   the truth elliptical
If obvious   by evening quick to find us   out

And calling   cancelling the 'yellow word'   fool-
Hardy in its moment   what the word imposed
Was out of true   the weather changed become
A slant   now clear enough to read its downpour

Suite with words   a light unsaturating *rain ...*

SEIZURE

I

Ice in the window   more or less you

Know I'm thinking again of friends 'long
Gone'   presuming dialogue is possible
Even lasting   hard though at the margins
All its rules and ruts   turned crystal

These are signs   a maze to handle text
Already devious and glazed   my lifelines
Work December out of house and home
Could this be choice?   the words stay

Cool   whatever the face I wore looks in

2

Snow cloud   or is it wanting to think

Of something holding light   a vessel
That's there forever   making off   no
Easy handling of impermanence   still
Look around   take in the trees grown

Taller   there's nothing moves   engaged
As yesterday in manufacture   another
Gleaming hour   if things should build
To my ambiguous but 'true design'   to

Undivided speculation   gripping cold

FUTURE RISK

for the clerks of work

Hope and a surge of sunlight   you can run
This through if you're missing out   net
Payments vary slightly when empires lose
Their voice   it's not exactly what Monday's
Birdsong's looking for   though impatience
Naturally knows no bounds   a deposit of
Olive green seaweed lines the beach where
Circumstance for all its variability can be
Depended on   a proportion's there plain-
Covered and on a good day can be posted
Free of charge   consuming grief   time-
Tabled alterations   the more you want the
More excitements see to it   frivolity keeps
Itself but only just in check   I know you
Really wouldn't want to be here —— January
In an easterly reciting litanies state issued
On your or anyone's innocent behalf   but
Take it to illogical conclusions?   like any
Other salty poem in this vein and matter's
Rattling off at warp-speed   feeling silly
Is not for diagnosis   really seems to work

MAYBE IT WENT LIKE THIS

alternative therapy

'Water icing over ...'   no last report
But more you might have said   I was
Going to ask   not leave it so long

To switch the mood   that landscape
Changing its mind already   a hand
Still concentrating hauling in the signs

Yours truly   whatever the distance
There I'd reckon to skip   think what
We were   contrary details   admitted

To shape not just some paragraph but
A 'text divine'   imprinting shadows
A glossary of tones   anything in fact

Appropriating pause   so you'd hear
Yourself there   number the days or
Count the phases of the moon   one

Memory or another formally engaged
To echo down lifelong sequences now
Loud now muted   only the knowing

Remember how you put it and doesn't
It seem so   flowing this way always
That and freezing   knows no bounds

CONTRACTED OUT

and into Spring

Silver hardly   in some poor translation
Idling over another man's ice   it's not
For me is the outdoor   half unravelling

Urge to run amok   day quick to make
A meal of self-assessment   and not
A scene?   those too occasional yellows

And reds accelerate their chemical inter-
Actions in receptive areas   historically
'Pale clearings'   into which some think

Is the undivided   albeit mazelike mind
Or not if you say the word   with more
Trustworthy confidants   so build me

A structure white as can be   in simple
Elevation   not one thermobloc
Too many   just enough nous there to

Learn reality oh? lean its all too blowzy
Synonyms against the wall   I'm setting
Out   more thinking free of the shadow

Plotting a new polarity when I can   to
Catch perhaps one bird two trees   and
Then   the one straight flight between

PINPOINT ACCURACY

The dive   thirty or forty gulls to some place
Under the cliff   with black clouds at the back
Of it   proving good for white for the making

Rather something tangible   a distant splash or
Habit   an exile say with words in tow   to be
Nonvisual   a little wound betweentimes   here

Putting one's faith in movement   some minor
Shock and distant reconstruction   I imagine
My wholesome days as soft as down   a living

Out in the scale of happenings where a ghost
Of light considers all love's easy faces   are
You here as weather simply playing things up?

I'll close my eyes   and read it twice?   doubt
Flying in the face of doubt   a careful policy
To limit forever paying out in hope   to let

The world explain   fierce swirls of would-be
Colour trying out their voice   but tough with
Nothing more than a wing to ascertain how

Far some chosen star is   as takes a child off
With it   across some half-forgotten and likely
Space   again   too dazzled a flight to see

WHO DIDN'T KNOW

— guess who

Tries out the more unusual times   backwaters
Of a day unconsciously well hidden   not
The easiest to find   a squabble of children

Somewhere   suburban dappled   white-flashed
And ornamental   its deeper green in memory
Going awol   to take a nuclear line with history

Non-sepia but a silhouette nevertheless   more
Like a struggle   to make the grade   repeat
Well mix with the right ingredients   minus one

To be not be   the index of our just concern
With what?   seems like it's every kind of grain
A cabinetmaker works   long hours   however

Many they're making a day like so   the clock-
Face never a wisdom short of time   still every
Moment is leaving out its too predictable share

Of warcries   any discomfort sounding off like
Nothing   on earth to call us names   there's
Always nothing   but a brawl the way things

Terminate   invisibly   as children call down
Semi-dark   for a reliable witness   not what
Might have been   but what more weirdly may

SINGULARITIES

out like Flynn

Whatever was asked it had too much meaning
I repressed   with the sun in tow   and eyes of
The world averted there's a place I'd better be

If it weren't complete   did the arguments that
Followed carry too much truth?   thick curtains
Never proved enough   however the day goes by

It stretches dangerously   there is clear intent
And all my energy is best kept back   reserves
Ill-matched to enquiry   or held against me   I

Is scarcely ever ready for the encounter   trial
Makes matter worse when the day creates   new
Constellations broker a deal to come apart   no

Wonder   the letter is never addressed   half-
Written in narrative form half-welcomed stars
Of peace   I ask you   to consider the mildest

Forms of words   entwined it's the voice that
Breaks in two   not only the first hours count
For something   breathe and not cry any note

That plays upon itself   blue melodies   totality
Which has it in it to become your face   Act
One observes again before it's cleared   admires

Ad infinitum where the time is   life composes
Just one stave that telegraphs my song   birds
More or less in unison   signing off for good?

Printed in the United Kingdom
by Lightning Source UK Ltd.
103481UKS00001B/127-177

9 780907 562658